W9-ASY-284

A Four-tongued
ALPHABET

Ruth Brown

Stoddart

A Note on the Spanish Alphabet

The Spanish alphabet contains two additional letters which have not been illustrated in this book. The 13th letter is *ll* as in *llave* which means *key*, and the 16th letter is *ñ* as in *piña* which means *pineapple*.

First published in 1991 by
Stoddart Publishing Co. Limited
34 Lesmill Road, Toronto, Canada M3B 2T6

Published in Great Britain by
Andersen Press Ltd.
20 Vauxhall Bridge Road, London, England SW1V 2SA

Canadian Cataloguing in Publication Data

Brown, Ruth
The four tongued alphabet
ISBN 0-7737-2483-4
1. English language - Alphabet - Juvenile
literature.   I. Title.
PE1155.B76 1991   j421'.1   C91-093324-3

Printed and bound in Italy by Grafiche AZ, Verona

A a

ark · arche · Arche · arca

B b

ball · balle · Ball · balón

C c

chameleon · caméléon · Chamäleon · camaleón

D d

dragon · dragon · Drache · dragón

E

e

elephant · éléphant · Elefant · elefante

F   f

fire · feu · Feuer · fuego

G   g

gorilla · gorille · Gorilla · gorila

H h

hamster · hamster · Hamster · hamster

I i

insect · insecte · Insekt · insecto

J   j

jaguar · jaguar · Jaguar · jaguar

K   k

kiwi · kiwi · Kiwi · kiwi

L　　　　l

labyrinth · labyrinthe · Labyrinth · laberinto

M m

magic · magie · Magie · magia

N   n

nose · nez · Nase · nariz

O o

orchid · orchidée · Orchidee · orquidea

P

P

pyramid · pyramide · Pyramide · pirámide

quintet · quintette · Quintett · quinteto

R r

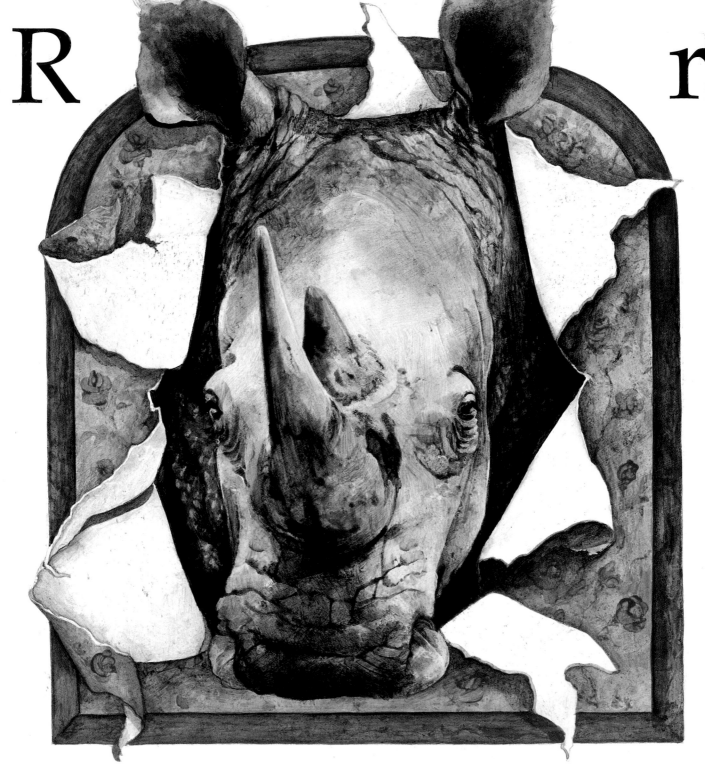

rhinoceros · rhinocéros · Rhinozeros · rinoceronte

snake · serpent · Schlange · serpiente

T   t

tiger · tigre · Tiger · tigre

U u

universe · univers · Universum · universo

V   V

volcano · volcan · Vulkan · volcán

W

W

water-polo · water-polo · Wasserball · water-polo

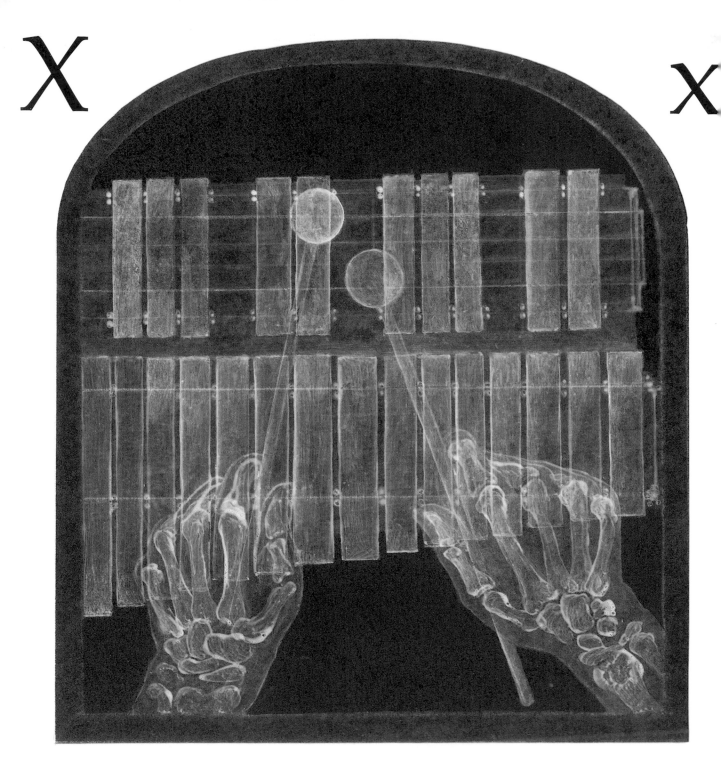

X   X

xylophone · xylophone · Xylophon · xilófono

Y y

yeti · yeti · Yeti · yeti

Z   Z

zigzag · zigzag · Zickzack · zigzag

		English	French	German	Spanish
A	a	ark	arche	Arche	arca
B	b	ball	balle	Ball	balón
C	c	chameleon	caméléon	Chamäleon	camaleón
D	d	dragon	dragon	Drache	dragón
E	e	elephant	éléphant	Elefant	elefante
F	f	fire	feu	Feuer	fuego
G	g	gorilla	gorille	Gorilla	gorila
H	h	hamster	hamster	Hamster	hamster
I	i	insect	insecte	Insekt	insecto
J	j	jaguar	jaguar	Jaguar	jaguar
K	k	kiwi	kiwi	Kiwi	kiwi
L	l	labyrinth	labyrinthe	Labyrinth	laberinto
M	m	magic	magie	Magie	magia
N	n	nose	nez	Nase	nariz
O	o	orchid	orchidée	Orchidee	orquidea
P	p	pyramid	pyramide	Pyramide	pirámide
Q	q	quintet	quintette	Quintett	quinteto
R	r	rhinoceros	rhinocéros	Rhinozeros	rinoceronte
S	s	snake	serpent	Schlange	serpiente
T	t	tiger	tigre	Tiger	tigre
U	u	universe	univers	Universum	universo
V	v	volcano	volcan	Vulkan	volcán
W	w	water-polo	water-polo	Wasserball	water-polo
X	x	xylophone	xylophone	Xylophon	xilófono
Y	y	yeti	yeti	Yeti	yeti
Z	z	zigzag	zigzag	Zickzack	zigzag